Grandma Edmons

From
Harlan & Mary

2-23-91

Bouquet of
Memories
From
the Heart

Published in the United States by Mark Publishing, 1990
ISBN 0-937769-15-0

Copyright ©1990
Produced by Mark Publishing
5400 Scotts Valley Drive
Scotts Valley, CA 95066

Poetry: **Frank Carpenter**
Illustrations: **Mary Ann Riemer**
Editor: **Judi Williams**
Design: **The Design Edge**

About the Author

Although he has been writing all his life, Frank Carpenter has only recently begun to write professionally. In this, his second book, he continues the warmth, insight and encouragement of the "Bouquet of Memories" series, capturing the beauty of simple situations and helping us to re-discover those feelings that seem to make every day so worth living. Frank has a heart for people and derives great satisfaction from helping others to express their own feelings through his work.

About the Artist

After retiring in 1979 from 21 years of teaching elementary school, Mary Ann Riemer began exploring painting with watercolors as a new hobby. Within a few years her natural talent turned her hobby into a full-time career. Mary Ann feels her work is a true expression of her deep appreciation of the world around her. Her art has been displayed in one-woman shows and on exhibit in several art galleries in Carmel and Santa Cruz, California.

This touching book is a singular event in fine bookmaking. It unites the talents of fellow artists Frank Carpenter and Mary Ann Riemer in a memorable collection of tender moments, enabling both artists to display their individual craft as well as work their collective magic.

For each of us, life is like
a bouquet of flowers.
Each memory of those you
love is a flower in the
bouquet of your life.
May the pages of this book
help to enhance the beauty
and fragrance of your
bouquet of memories.

Love has
many forms and faces
and we can
always find new ways
to show love
to the
people in our lives . . .

Warm Gesture

When I was sick the other day
and lonely as could be,
you made a batch of homemade soup
and came to visit me.

You stayed awhile, and it felt good
just to pass the time of day.
Before you left you served the soup
and brought it on a tray.

And later, after you had gone
and left the steaming bowl,
the aroma of your gesture
still warmed my heart and soul.

Real Love

It isn't very difficult
to say what you may feel
but only through your actions
can you prove your love is real.

The Lesson

My car ran out of gas one day,
what was I to do?
Twenty miles from a phone,
then suddenly I saw you.

Frantically I waved and tried
to get you to slow down,
without a second thought you stopped
and drove me into town.

Along the way we talked a bit,
and I began to find
you made me feel so comfortable
by being warm and kind.

When we arrived I bought some gas
and a can to put it in.
Then right away you volunteered
to drive me back again.

So now when someone else needs help,
I'll stop to help them too.
For love is more than something said . . .
it's something that you do.

Response

It's easy to love
when you are loved,
and give when you receive . . .
but the truest love
springs in response
to those who are in need.

Thank You

Thank you for being a friend to me
when I needed a friend like you.
Thank you for your sound advice
when I didn't know what to do.

Thank you for lending a shoulder
when I needed a place to cry.
Thank you for giving a gentle nudge
when I just didn't want to try.

Thank you for being all the things
I could want a friend to be
and for all the ways that you have found
to show your love for me.

The Best that I can Be

You love me so much
that I could stay
just the way I am today...
but you never give up
encouraging me
to be the best that I can be.

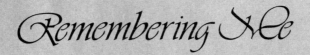

Remembering Me

May I never be remembered
for the size of my estate . . .
the places that I've traveled
or some other worldly trait . . .

For the things that I've collected
and the things that I have made,
may be squandered or discarded
or be left to rust or fade.

Rather let me be remembered
for the way that I have cared . . .
for the people I've assisted
and the love that I have shared.

If I am to be remembered
judge me not by work or play . . .
not by the things I purchased
but the love I gave away.

Just Because

I really didn't expect it
but there the letter was.
When I read my mail I found it . . .
you sent it just because.
Thank you for your gesture.
You knew just what to say
to lift my spirits instantly,
and brighten up my day.

Tenderness

Love can be compassion
or opening your home.
Love may be some needed cash
or just calling on the phone.

Love might be shown by listening
or a sparkle in your eye . . .
Love can be most anything
It simply means you try.

Hospitality

When I needed to find a place
where people cared for me,
I was welcomed by your warmth
and your hospitality.

Glimmer of Hope

A child watches his own front door
just about six o'clock,
the puppy wags his tail and begs
ready for his walk.

A young man knocks on his date's front door
wondering what to say,
toddlers clamor around on the floor
begging for someone to play.

The soup-kitchen line is filled with folks
just hoping to get a meal,
a street boy wants to shine your shoes
promising you a "good deal".

At work and home most everywhere
with a glimmer of hope in their eyes,
there are people who need you and your love . . .
won't you listen to their cries?

Romance
has a
special magic and wonder
all its own . . .

Quiet Man

I'm a strong, but quiet man,
not the kind to say
the things a woman longs to hear . . .
I'm just not made that way.

It's true, you are a quiet man
and though your words are few,
the ones you pick are chosen well
to let your love shine through.

By My Side

Boundless is my love for you ...
endless is my pride.
I'm honored knowing that you'll be
forever by my side.

With the Dew

Early I wake,
turning to find you dreaming by my side.
Softly I kiss
your brow as I hold you close, my bride.
Gently I rise
being careful not to waken you.
Early I wake,
and leave you dreaming with the morning dew.

Quiet Moments

In quiet moments
just near dusk
when all is calm about,
I know you are the only thing
I cannot live without.

Just as the dawn
begins to glow
when day springs fresh and new,
I hold you tightly
in my arms . . .
and lose myself in you.

Pastel Shades

Pastel shades envelop me
within a quiet room.
Curtains dance with ocean breezes
playing sultry tunes.
As we share together
your love surrounds me so.
The world outside seems far away . . .
this moment is all I know.

Near Me

Across the room I'm watching you
absorbed in some good book.
And though I'm very near to you,
you don't notice when I look.

I glance at you from time to time
for though I know you're there,
it comforts me to see you near
and know how much you care.

Your thoughts are busy elsewhere
for your day was long and rough,
there's so much I want to tell you
but your presence is enough.

It isn't what you say to me
nor all the things you do,
it's just the quiet confidence
I get from loving you.

Bright Tomorrows

I see us walking down the beach
together, hand in hand.
And as we stroll the waves erase
our footprints in the sand.

Strangely, we don't seem to care
about what's left behind.
The sights and sounds that lie ahead
all occupy our minds.

We've shared so many memories
more often joys than sorrows.
But our best years are yet to come
all filled with bright tomorrows.

Still Burning

The fire still burns brightly
and though your hair is gray,
the beauty that I see in you
grows deeper every day.

Even though my eyes are dim
I still can clearly see,
that happy day so long ago
when love found you and me.

A Walk in the Park

I saw an older couple
walking in the park today . . .
talking softly to each other
as they watched the children play.

I noticed that he held her hand
and stood like he was proud . . .
then some private joke she said
made them both laugh out loud.

And I laughed too, for even though
I couldn't hear their jest,
it warmed my heart to see romance
in bloom and at its best.

And I realized that these two
just like folks who are alone,
together now were reaping
the life that they had sown.

The Rose and I

Pressed in the pages of a book
on some high and dusty place,
a withered rose lays silently
within the book's embrace.

I never gave that rose to you
for I was far too shy.
You never knew the way I felt,
only the rose . . . and I.

Just for Me

Is there someone out there
who is waiting just for me?
Should I go out and find him
or just wait patiently?

I have waited all my life
for love to come my way.
Will I be disappointed?
Will I have my special day?

I believe that day will come
when somehow, suddenly
I'll find the special person
who is waiting just for me!

Symphony

*Each heart is a musical instrument
and has a special tone
that never seems to sound quite right
if played all alone.*

But when hearts come together
the way they're meant to be,
the love they share bursts forth into
a beautiful symphony.

*Most often
love is
learned and lived
within our families...*

Good Investment

As a matter of good business,
I try to find a way
to show a little kindness
to my loved ones every day.

It's a very small investment,
and through the years I've learned ...
when I show simple interest,
my investment is returned.

The love and kindness I invest
in those I care about,
compounds each day 'till there's so much
I never will run out.

Day's End

In the evenings when the children
are all sleeping in their beds,
and after we have kissed them
upon their sleepy heads...
when all the dinner dishes
are dried and stacked away,
and the blocks and books and puzzles
have been picked up for the day...
then the kettle starts to singing
saying, "have a cup of tea,"
and the fire dances gaily
as it beckons you and me.
In those quiet hours
when we talk and sing and read,
our hearts are drawn together...
it's a special time indeed.

Stowaway

My job requires travel
so quite often I'm not home.
I love my family dearly
and it's hard to be alone.

But my dear wife has a custom
that may not seem like much,
and though it seems a silly game,
it helps keep us in touch.

Whenever I am packing
for a trip she secretly
slips some small card or present
in my case where I can't see.

Well, just knowing that it's in there
makes it easier to go,
and reminds me of my family
much more than you will know.

She does it every time I leave
so what I always do . . .
as I'm going out the door
I leave her something too.

The Heart of a Child

When I was young I didn't care
how people looked or talked.
I was oblivious to how
they dressed and how they walked.
Oh, to have a child's love . . .
the kind that sets me free,
to love someone for what's inside
and not for what I see.

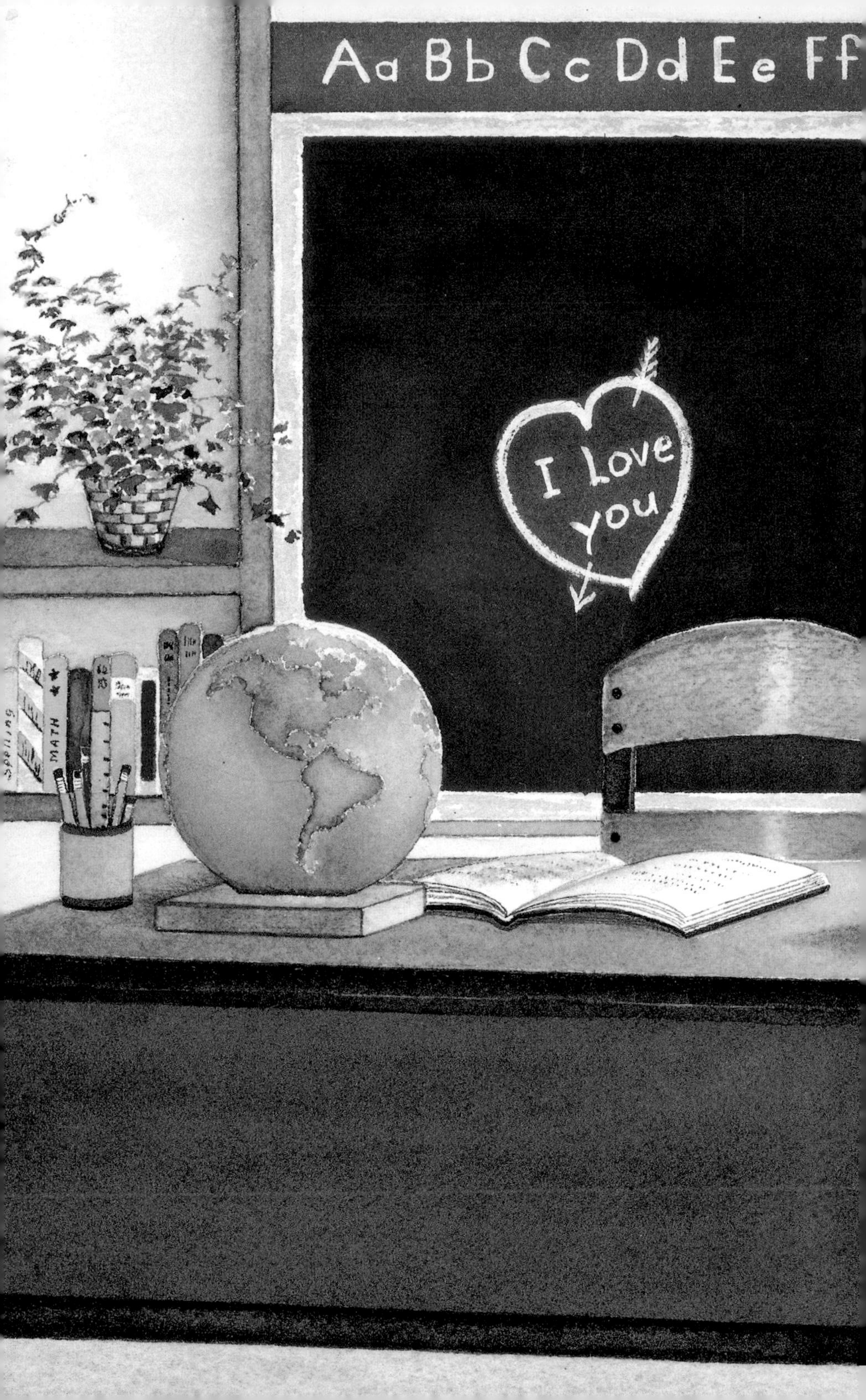
Aa Bb Cc Dd Ee Ff
I Love you
MATH
Spelling

g Hh Ii Jj Kk Ll Mm Nn Oo P

First Love

Cupid's arrow struck me first
while I was still in school,
long before I understood
love's fundamental rules.

And like so many other youths
I could not understand
just why my love was not returned
the way that I had planned.

So if you've ever had a crush
upon a teacher too,
you certainly are not alone . . .
I was just like you.

My Best Friend

Lots of people love me
and they always tell me so.
But someone loves me most of all,
much more than you could know.

Of course he never says it,
but only 'cause he can't . . .
still I can see it in his eyes,
the way he smiles and pants.

He wakes me up for school each day
and tucks me in at night.
He even sleeps right by my bed
in case I have a fright.

Sure, I love my parents
just like any child would do.
But especially I love my dog,
and you would love him too.

My Dad

You ask
who is the best friend
that I really ever had?
That's an easy one to answer
'cause I love him . . .
he's my dad!

Passing it On

"We lost our kite,"
I told my dad,
"it's stuck up in that tree."
"Let me see what I can do,"
he said and winked at me.
Then instantly he climbed to where
the kite was stuck up top.
He expertly untangled it
and gently let it drop.

That night my little sister
needed help to tie her shoe.
I winked at her and said,
"let me see what I can do."

Honesty

Whenever I ask a question,
the answer I receive
may not be the one I want to hear,
but it's the one I can believe.
So loving you is easy
since you tell the truth to me.
We always know just where we stand
because of honesty.

Comfort

I'm old, my strength has faded
and I find it hard to walk.
Lately, I have even found
it's difficult to talk.
So everyone ignores me
as if I wasn't there,
and even my own family
seldom seem to care.
But you treat me differently,
I think you understand.
You take the time to sit with me
and simply hold my hand.

We hope this collection of memories will encourage you to make the most of each new day and enjoy those you love to the fullest. May your bouquet of memories continue to grow and flourish so that it's fragrance fills your life with joy.